BOOKS BY

KAY AMBROSE

THE BALLET-LOVER'S POCKET-BOOK (1945)

THE BALLET-LOVER'S COMPANION (1949)

THE BALLET-STUDENT'S PRIMER (1954)

These are BORZOI BOOKS

Published by ALFRED A. KNOPF, *in New York*

THE BALLET-STUDENT'S PRIMER

Celia
Franca as
Queen of
the Wilis
in "Giselle"

T H E

BALLET-STUDENT'S
PRIMER

A Concentrated
Guide for Beginners
of All Ages

by KAY AMBROSE

IN COLLABORATION WITH

CELIA FRANCA

NEW YORK

ALFRED A. KNOPF

1 9   8 4

L. C. catalog card number: 54-8756

THIS IS A BORZOI BOOK,
PUBLISHED BY ALFRED A. KNOPF, INC.

Copyright 1953 by KAY AMBROSE. All rights reserved under International and Pan-American Copyright Conventions. Published in the United States by Alfred A. Knopf, Inc., New York and distributed by Random House, Inc., New York. Manufactured in the United States of America.

Published October 18, 1954
Reprinted Seventeen Times
Nineteenth Printing, February 1984

Published in Great Britian by A. & C. Black, Ltd. under the title of BEGINNERS, PLEASE!

CONTENTS

THE BALLET-STUDENT'S PRIMER

INTRODUCTION

1. INTRODUCTION TO BALLET AS A MAJOR ART

Dancing is something more than one of the arts—basically it is one of the instincts, and its history started long before there were any historians to write about it. Probably in its most ancient form it was ritualistic, but even then it must have been performed with conscious decorative intent. *Real* dancing is "that dance which is as the very heartbeats of universal life" and, in the form of ballet, it is subject to all the rules which govern the great classical arts.

For instance, you cannot reasonably expect to become a great composer unless you study how to handle an orchestra, the various instruments, musical notation, and the works of the great composers who have gone before you. To become a great painter you must study perspective, anatomy and architecture. A prospective poet must have a complete mastery of his language, an impeccable sense of rhythm and great visionary gifts. To become a great dancer you must have some, at least, of all these qualities, and the greatest dancers are the ones that have the most.

We must leave the study of genius out of this brief summary of dancing because a genius is a person who can sense, reproduce, or perform things he has never been taught. Here we are concerned with the identification of a certain school of art, that of the classical ballet, which has its origin deeply rooted in the ancient dances mentioned above, and which, in common with all the classical arts, demands complete dedication from its exponents; which makes full use of every device known to the theatre; and which cannot exist in its final form without the arts of music and painting, with which it is fused.

Ballet, then, is a triple art, made from dancing, music, and painting combined. If one of these elements is over-emphasised, disregarded, or misunderstood, the whole effect becomes unbalanced and spoilt. Throughout its several hundred years of existence, ballet has suffered certain relapses into vulgarity, disrepute, over-production and over-civilisation; but it has survived a transition from the courts of kings and rulers, through the lowest music-halls, to become a great national art-form which is enriching the culture of many countries. Now, it has to survive the dangers of over-popularity as an entertainment, and another more subtle menace: a fine ballet company, which has no language barrier, has been recognised as a magnificent asset to increase international prestige. Let us hope that all governments will have the sense to make dancers ambassadors of international goodwill only, and not try to make ballet the vehicle for political ideas. When all is said and done, history has shown that political content is always fatal to art, just as genuine religious inspiration has always proved the greatest stimulant—a highly unfashionable admission, but of undeniable truth.

To return to the three main components of ballet (it is necessary to insist that there are three components, although a critic has just complained that this insistence is "boring"!). Although the study of music and painting is very desirable for the prospective dancer, it is the third element, that of the basic technique of the classical ballet itself, which it is the hardest to establish. It is comparatively easy to lay down laws and precepts concerning musicians and painters, for we can always refer to great paintings and musical works to bear out what we want to say, or to preach; but dancing—! When the dancer has danced, the only thing which remains of the performance is— the length of time it will live in the minds of those who saw it.

Luckily, however, a school of dancing is another matter, for

that is concerned with an element which can lead to a genera-
tion of brilliant dancers—namely, the cultivation of an artistic
standard, which can live, grow, and develop for ever.

2. THE PROFESSIONAL APPROACH

I wonder if there is anybody who has not at one time
or another wondered what it would be like to float through the
air like the immortal Pavlova; grip the imagination, like Nijin-
sky; with sparkling eyes and flawless technique, dazzle like
Kschessinskaya? alternately, cajole and command, like Karsa-
vina, or play with the audience, like Babilée?

Some might comment "What *fun!*"—disregarding the years
of toil attached to these delightful powers.

Some might answer with a sigh: "That would be a dream,"
and here, indeed, we have the more realistic approach of the
two. The secret of the realisation of the dream is that *it must
be a vision which can also be perceived by an audience.* Most
of us have dreamed that we were flying, and sighed to remember
the delicious and unearthly sensation the following morning;
but Pavlova, who managed to keep her poetic interpretative
powers unbruised by the drudgery of theatrical tours and the
hard technical work of the classroom, was able to project the
illusion of flying to those who saw her dance. Galina Ulanova
seems to have achieved the same almost hypnotic power in
Russia to-day.

So the first conscious realisation of ballet is in full accordance with the ancient belief that dancing must be a wholly
unselfish art. A sentimental journey is no good in the theatre
unless you can take your audience with you (after all, they
have paid for their seats), and to watch a dancer who is enjoy-
ing herself in her own way, without reference to theatrical
interpretation, is like watching a sleeper who has a smile on her
face, and wondering what she is dreaming about.

The first step towards a sensitive and professional stage performance of ballet is bound up with the first steps of the

student in the classroom, and it is with these preliminary movements that this little book is concerned.

3. FOR THE BEGINNER

Of the two predecessors to this volume, the *Ballet-Lover's Pocket-Book* is specially designed for the use of ballet audiences and casual experimenters, as it includes simplified explanations of the main phenomena concerning a ballet performance. The *Ballet-Lover's Companion*, written after the *Pocket-Book*, is for the use of the more advanced student and for the ballet connoisseur, and contains illustrated examples relating to the æsthetic training of the dancer. It seems, however, from all accounts, that both these books are being used as practical primers by all sorts of dancers, and this is a purpose for which they were not altogether intended.

In response to a general demand, therefore, I set about compiling a small book for the use of ballet beginners, again selecting Celia Franca as my collaborator. Miss Franca's extraordinary gifts as a dancer are only equalled by her talents as a teacher of ballet, a combination which is unusual enough to be remarkable. Which of the great dancers mentioned earlier in this chapter have left us a legacy of outstanding pupils? Great dancers there are who have made great teachers, but they are few indeed.

My aim has been to assemble the bare bones of elementary ballet (there isn't room for any frills), and, of course, the worst difficulty has been to decide what material might safely be omitted. A more advanced book on ballet might well have been an easier task, as in that case one addresses students whom one assumes are already acquainted with posture, and what to wear under their tights. Nevertheless, it should be possible for dance students of all ages to use the information included in this small book with safety. It is not intended as a preparation for any particular examination in ballet, but is designed to be of practical assistance to boys and girls who have perforce to work at home; and as for the luckier ones who are attending classes, it may well serve them as a reference book and help them towards a better understanding of what their ballet master or mistress is trying to teach them. But I hope sincerely that the number of ballet beginners who are unable to reach a class of any description will be few indeed.

In other words, although this book is not intended to take the place of a teacher of dancing, it is, however, an abbreviated primer. It gives a general idea of the sequence and purpose of a normal, preliminary ballet class, and it is freely addressed to that army of ballet-lovers which forms the backbone of any audience, including photographers, artists, columnists, and general connoisseurs.

The exercises shown here may seem rather dull, but, as you will find, they are surprisingly difficult; and if you master all the movements and poses and then perform them in the correct order the right number of times—*i.e.*, if you "do a class" lasting approximately an hour—you will certainly have achieved a good deal. As any dancer will tell you, doing a class on your own is very hard and difficult work even if you are already familiar with all the steps; however, do your best (working out the tempo will probably be the most awkward if you have no one to help you), and when you do visit a ballet class you won't find yourself entirely lost.

On pages 78–79 I have indicated two advanced steps just so that you can keep in mind what may be your ultimate reward. But try not to grow too impatient—to run before you can walk is a most risky affair.

4. TO THE TEACHER

Just take a look at the contents of the average ballet classroom and then glance at the pictures of immortal dancers which usually decorate the studio walls. You are the person who has undertaken the miracle of turning one into the other, and this metamorphosis can only take place under your direct supervision, never from the pages of a book.

You will be the first to recognise the difficulties presented in compiling this small volume, where I have found myself thoroughly hedged in by a number of limitations, including lack of space. You must have found in the course of dance-training, part of which features the correction of faults in natural figure construction, that it is by a thousand subtle methods that you accustom the different dancers to master the difficult ballet technique and to recognise and respond to the different moods and timing of music, bearing in mind that some future choreographer will be using those same students to express his ballets. How can such subtleties be included in any book, let alone one of this time? The answer is, of course, that the subtleties of the dancer's training are entirely up to you.

The selection of steps, exercises, and the drawings of basic poses in these pages are adapted from a system which has proved to be a successful one, and which includes steps and information from various well-known methods of dancing.

For the information of the general reader, it must be strongly emphasised that a good teach is always one who obtains excellent results from any system he or she has devised or adopted. A good system of dance-training—Cecchetti, Royal Academy of Dancing, Russian, etc.—is a good system no longer if indifferently taught.

5. FOR PARENTS AND GUARDIANS

i. THE PROBLEM CHILD

For the parents of a really determined would-be dancer, ballet can be a grim subject. Most parents have no objection to a child taking ballet lessons as a part of a general education; but when the young person in question shows in no uncertain manner that he or she is absolutely resolved to take up professional ballet as a career, in very many cases some alarming problems present themselves. For instance, there is the awful uncertainty of height; for a girl, five foot six inches is the danger line. She must be prepared to start work seriously as from the age of ten, or at the latest, twelve: will she study ballet at the expense of some of her general education, and then grow too tall to make a first-rate dancer; or perhaps, suddenly lose interest?

At the very outset of this discussion one thing must be made abundantly clear. All uncertainties, including height, talent, strength, and opportunities, are offset by one significant certainty—that whereas the serious study of ballet will bring about increased poise and self-possession for the student, there is ample evidence that to refuse to allow a determined child to study dancing will result in a very real frustration in later years, and it will then be too late to cure it.

As to the always vexed question, whether a child is really serious over a career in ballet or merely dazzled by films and star performances: an excellent test is to deliver a strong dose of ballet classes with a good teacher. As a rule, the teacher will be able to diagnose the seriousness and talent of the student; and anyway, the hard training for a ballet dancer will soon grow monotonous to any but the serious student, and will cure in record time someone who is merely stage-struck.

ii. CHOICE OF TEACHER

This is a very serious matter indeed, as a mistake can be as far-reaching in its results as a wrong choice of medical advice. The best way of ensuring that a teacher is a reputable one is to communicate with one of the best known Teachers' Associations, which will be allied to one or more of the most famous and approved methods of dancing, some of which are referred to in these pages.

Parents should also bear in mind that endless displays and recitals by young students are not necessarily indicative of good ballet training. It may be all very well for those who wish to pursue the more commercial side of stage entertainment, but perpetual displays by tiny tots and young students should be regarded rather as an advertising campaign by a commercially minded teacher than as good experience for the pupils. One recital a year is quite enough for any teacher, mother, or student: remember that the greatest teachers of dancing give a students' recital once in a blue moon, if ever. Once again, tradition has shown that premature stage appearances merely tend to make ballet pupils unduly conceited, and encourage the teacher to believe in his or her perfections as a "choreographer"—a much misunderstood word, now used to describe the efforts of anyone who attempts to arrange dances of any kind. So remember—although a ballet dancer must be good to be commercially successful, it doesn't work the other way round.

The danger of sending a child to a bad teacher cannot be over-stressed. It is my painful duty to place on record that there are very many cases of children who, showing remarkable talent, have been allowed to study for some time with a bad teacher; the parents, at last discovering that the teacher was not *bona fide*, have taken the child away and sent it to a qualified one, but often too late. The second teacher has had the heartbreaking task of telling the parents that the child has been physically ruined, and can never be cured of the effects of a really shocking start.

Allowing a child to rise on her *pointes* before she is ready is one of the most outstanding examples of bad training; but there are a thousand physical maladjustments which may take place as a result of improper instruction—none of which would be noticed by any but an expert in its early stages. So be warned!

A qualified teacher is a person who can and should be approached on every matter concerning the serious student's welfare, including what sports and recreations may be studied without spoiling the ideal dancer's physique—and also upon the important question of *shoes*. Don't buy footwear advertised as "ballet shoes" in any store, and run the risk of ruining the child's feet. Take the teacher's advice and if necessary send for the scientifically made shoes which have been developed and improved for several hundred years to help protect and strengthen the feet in the right way.

Whereas no trouble should be spared to find the right teacher for the prospective ballet student, many parents and guardians may be glad to have certain information before starting the search. I will therefore include a few basic facts which should be taken in the same spirit as the drawings of technical ballet steps which follow: they are addressed to those people who want to obtain a general idea of the subject before approaching an expert.

Age and height. In the case of children who are under seven years of age, "dancing classes" composed of little steps accompanied by nursery rhymes and other simple tunes are more suitable than ballet classes. Children under seven are not usually physically or mentally ready for the rigorous ballet training, except in the most extraordinary cases.

At the age of twelve to thirteen a girl is usually considered too old to commence training and become a really excellent dancer. Nevertheless girls have been known who have started at fourteen and have made successful careers.

Boys are fundamentally stronger physically than girls and can start their training later, but not later than fourteen if they are to make excellent dancers. But it must be placed on record that one very famous dancer started his training at the age of twenty-two.

As to height: for girls, five foot six is the usual limit, but taller dancers have been known who have made extremely successful careers. In a young child, long hands and feet are danger signals, being usually an indication of height to come, but not invariably so.

Preliminary study. (The following information is exclusive of tiny tots and infant prodigies.

i. For a preliminary student, two classes a week of one hour each constitutes the average.

ii. During this class, *all* the exercises given in this book for the *barre* should be performed. (Naturally, a beginner would take some weeks at least to learn the movements, quite a time to grow accustomed to them, and—in keeping with ballet as a whole—the rest of his life trying to perfect them!)

iii. Still in the course of that hour, in the second part of the class known as *centre practice,* separate attention should be given to the exercises listed under that heading; bearing in mind that it is better to improve two exercises than to rush through too many steps imperfectly. Time should always be left for at least one *adage* and some *allégro* before the hour is over.

It should be noted that no student is expected to master all the steps shown in this book in his or her first few visits to the classroom. All the material shown is elementary, and it may be mastered in the time specified by the teacher. The *pointe*-work shown is preliminary, but can only be attempted after training in soft practice shoes is complete and approved by the teacher. In fact—

iv. *No pointe-work should be attempted until at least two years of study are complete.*

It should then only take place under the guidance of a qualified teacher.

No child should be permitted to rise on her *pointes* until she has passed her tenth year. If she takes her first class when she is ten, she must under no circumstances try *pointe-work* until two years later, when she is twelve, and so on.

v. For parents who wish to know how much time it would be necessary to devote to ballet training for a child of, say, ten years, who is to become a serious student with a view to a professional career: the approximate amount of study would be as follows. For the first two years, two classes a week as described; then three to four classes a week (strength and homework permitting) until the child reaches the age of thirteen; then every day until school-leaving age. Arrangements for free time in which to attend ballet classes can be made with most present-day schools, which have an enlightened attitude towards children who have obvious careers before them.

vi. Regarding technical terms in ballet: these are mostly in French, and as part of every student's training naturally consists of ballet "theory," these terms may present something of a stumbling block to some young people. There is little space in this book to pursue the derivations of the French terms, and none to arrange a system of phonetic pronunciation: so I have indicated the approximate meanings only. For exact translations and pronunciation the best course would be to secure a small French dictionary, which usually gives some general system for phonetic pronunciation in the introductory matter, and in which the words used in ballet can be found and identified.

The value of learning these French terms at the outset of one's ballet education is obvious. Their use in training is international, and with their help one may study ballet coherently with a teacher in any country in the world—even if one doesn't understand a word of the language used outside the classroom.

vii. There are many uses for each step, position, and movement, but partly from lack of space and partly to retain simplicity the main uses only are indicated.

No single method of dancing has been adhered to. The exercises are elementary, are an aggregate of various methods, and if carefully followed will not impart to the students any tricks or habits which will render them unsuitable to continue training with any good teacher of ballet.

Preliminary advice

FOR A BEGINNER'S BALLET CLASS:

"Begin at the beginning," the King said gravely,
"and go on till you come to the end: then stop."

—*The King of Hearts in* ALICE IN WONDERLAND

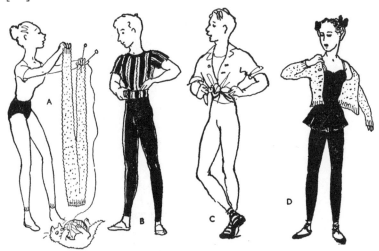

I. COSTUMES FOR CLASS

The main purpose of wearing tights for class is to keep the legs warm. More injuries result from cold muscles than from any other cause. Tights are usually worn without feet attached as they last longer this way, but ankle socks are always worn inside practice shoes. Sketch A: a girl knitting a pair of tights. They may be kept up with an elastic at the waist, or by rolling the top round a belt; or, for boys, by elastic "braces" (see Sketch I below). D shows the regulation tunic and tights favoured by many schools. E, another version of the same; F, a girl's jersey leotard, usually worn

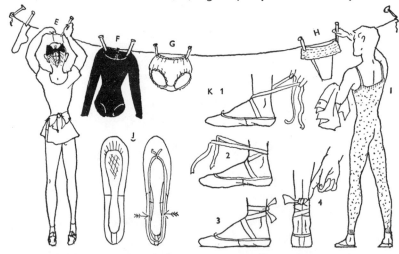

over tights; G, panties, usually worn by girls over tights and in conjunction with a sweater or shirt; H, a "dance belt" as worn by boys
under tights. J, two views of the regulation soft ballet shoe—*don't
purchase any other type of footwear for ballet*. K—for girls only;
how to tie ballet shoe ribbons (4, tie a knot and tuck the ends out
of sight). Boys sometimes wear their shoes with an elastic sewn
over the instep, sometimes they can keep them on without any
help. L and M, two people suitably dressed for class; the teacher
will be able to see and correct every line and muscle of the body.
N and O—the reverse. NEVER go to a ballet class dressed like this;
even the angles of your head will be hidden by all that fuzz of hair.
R, a terrible *arabesque* in a terrible costume; Q, a nice *arabesque*
in a suitable costume. P, if you have occasion to practise in slacks,
all right—but look out for the cuffs. Frightful accidents have hap-
pened this way. Bicycle clips round the ankles are some safeguard.

DANGER!!

II. EXERCISES À LA BARRE

i. *PRELIMINARY NOTES*

The following exercises for the *barre*, performed in the order given, are the correct and scientific way of warming up the body, loosening the joints and setting the circulation in motion before centre practice takes place. Each exercise should be performed the number of times indicated.

"Limbering"—stretching, kicking, etc.—is very dangerous until the body is "warmed up" by *barre* exercises. Warmth in this sense has nothing to do with the weather.

Careful study of the drawings will show that the *barre* exercises contain bits of the more showy and glamorous exercises given later for centre practice.

The instructions given with each series of sketches have been kept at an absolute minimum. The sketches have been made with a great deal of care, however, and the straight knees, well turned out from the thighs, the deportment, and the alert and pleasant expression of the figures should be copied, even if attention is not drawn to these details in the accompanying text.

The *barre*, usually to be found round the walls of a class-room, is about 3 ft. 6 ins. from the floor. There are sometimes other *barres* of various heights underneath, suitable for youthful performers. At home, a chair back is a good substitute for a *barre*; if you place too much pressure on it, it will simply overbalance, and you with it.

The black and white costumes on the sketched figures are to make it easier to follow the separate movements of the right and left sides. To "read" the sketches: turn this book upside down and place it on the floor in front of you, when the right and left sides of the sketched figures will correspond with your own.

" Turn this book
upside down — "

ii. THE FIVE BASIC POSITIONS OF THE FEET: BASIC DEPORTMENT

(*Above, right*) The five basic positions of the feet should be memorised in the first instance by the prospective dancer, as training cannot begin without them. In all positions the feet should be turned out from the hip, as this gives greater freedom for all types of movement. Beginners should not force their legs to turn out too greatly at first, as this usually results in rolling ankles. All the toes should be flat on the floor. If, for example, too much weight is taken on the big toe, the arch of the foot will be seen to flatten, which weakens the instep. In all positions when the heels are flat on the ground, the weight of the body should be shared equally by both legs.

The correct distribution of the weight of the body is dependent on right posture at the *barre*. In Sketch A1 below, note how a stupid dancer, in an attempt to force her feet to turn out, has rolled her ankles forward and relaxed her knees (which has pushed out her bottom), and attempted to put matters right by arching her back, sticking out her ribs, and lifting her chin. 2 shows a faulty posture typical of many beginners, characterised by stooping shoulders. Both these dancers are relying far too much on the support of the *barre*. 3 shows the ideal posture—straight knees, all muscles pulled upward so that the body has a slim line, and the hand resting lightly on the *barre*. Care should be taken not to place the hand too far back on the *barre*, as this twists the shoulder. B, an example of the way weight distribution is controlled when shifting from one position to another. C1, a foot half stretched. 2, three-quarters stretched. 3, fully stretched. 4, *sur la pointe*. D, a turned-in version of B. *Don't do this.*

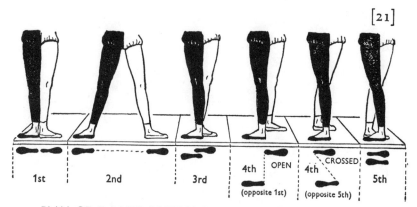

PLAN OF 5 BASIC POSITIONS OF THE FEET

1st   2nd   3rd   4th OPEN (opposite 1st)   4th CROSSED (opposite 5th)   5th

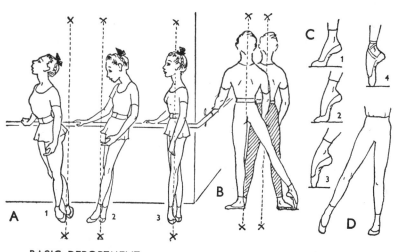

BASIC DEPORTMENT

BRIEF ENGLISH
TRANSLATIONS
OF TERMS
SHOWN BELOW

1st · TENDU TO THE SECOND · 2nd · TENDU TO THE SECOND · 3rd

1 2 3 4 5 6 7 8 9 10 11

SHIFT WEIGHT
OF BODY AS
TOE MOVES

11. EN TROISIÈME
10. PLIÉ EN TROISIEME
9. EN TROISIÈME   3rd position
8. TENDU À LA SECONDE
7. EN SECONDE   2nd position
6. PLIÉ EN SECONDE
5. EN SECONDE
4. TENDU À LA SECONDE
3. EN PREMIÈRE
2. PLIÉ EN PREMIÈRE
1. EN PREMIÈRE   1st position

START
HERE

III. BEGINNER'S CLASS: FIRST HALF

i. *PLIÉS AT THE BARRE IN ALL POSITIONS OF THE FEET*

Before attempting any exercise, care should be taken to ensure that the posture is correct (according to instructions on the previous page). The free arm (in this case, the right one) should have the elbow lifted and not be allowed to hug the side of the waist. The outside of the little finger should be allowed to touch the front of the thigh.

During the time devoted to assuming the correct posture the mind should also be schooled so that the exercise is performed intelligently and consciously. In other words—think what you are doing.

"*Plié*" is from the verb *plier*, to bend. One of the main purposes of the exercise is flexibility of the knees. If these are held well back, the

TENDU TO THE 4th OPEN · 4th OPEN · TENDU TO THE 4th OPEN · 5th · TENDU TO THE 4th CROSSED · 4th CROSSED

12 13 14 15 16 17 18 19 20 21 22 23

REPEAT EXERCISE FACING OTHER WAY

Always turn towards the barre

12. TENDU À LA QUATRIÈME (OUVERTE)
13. EN QUATRIÈME (OUVERTE) — 4th position open
14. PLIÉ EN QUATRIÈME (OUVERTE)
15. EN QUATRIÈME (OUVERTE)
16. TENDU À LA QUATRIÈME (OUVERTE)
17. EN CINQUIÈME — 5th position
18. PLIÉ EN·CINQUIÈME
19. EN·CINQUIÈME
20. TENDU À LA QUATRIÈME DEVANT (CROISÉE)
21. EN QUATRIÈME CROISÉE — 4th position closed
22. PLIÉ EN QUATRIÈME (CROISÉE)
23. EN QUATRIÈME CROISÉE

hip joints are loosened and the muscles of the groin stretched (which is already an aid to achieving a good "turn-out" of the whole leg). Indicated on this page are erect figures in the basic positions of the feet and a full *plié* in each one. Sinking to the lowest point in a *plié*, the student should pass through the quarter and *demi-plié* positions indicated on the following page. As an exercise, two *pliés* should be executed in each position, using two bars of slow waltz time to go down, and two to come up. The change from one foot position to another is accomplished by means of a (*battement*) *tendu*, as shown by the pin-men across the top of this double page.

The *tendu* to the next position is taken quickly so that the student can start the next *plié* on the first beat of the bar. When the exercise is finished with the right leg, turn round and repeat it the other way.

At all times the back must be held erect.

A

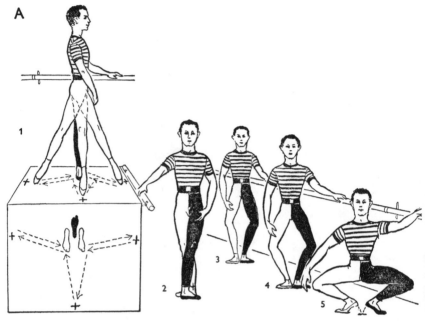

"EN CROIX" (BATTEMENTS TENDUS)
USUAL POSITION À LA BARRE:
QUARTER, DEMI, AND FULL PLIÉS

B

BATTEMENTS TENDUS EN CROIX

ii. "EN CROIX": BATTEMENTS TENDUS: GRANDS BATTEMENTS

Fig. A1 shows a man doing *battements tendus en croix*. *"En croix"* means "in the shape of a cross" and the term can apply to many exercises. An exercise *en croix* is always performed thus: to the front, closing front; to the side, closing behind; to the back, closing behind; to the side, closing front (see sequence B, below). A2 shows the front view of the student standing in 5th position at the *barre*, the preliminary for many exercises. 3 shows a quarter *plié*, 4 a *demi* (or half) *plié*, 5 a full *plié*, all in the first position of the feet.

B. *Battements tendus* mean "stretched beatings." The main purpose of the exercise is to stretch and strengthen the insteps. In the execution, the whole leg should be turned outwards from the thigh so that when the working foot is in 4th front (B2) the heel is forced upwards; in the 2nd (to the side, B4), the heel is forced forwards; in 4th, at the back (B6), the heel is pushed down towards the ground.

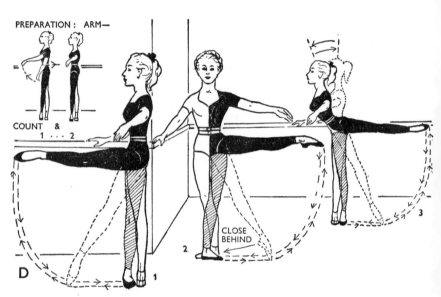

C

BATTEMENTS TENDUS WITH DEMI-PLIÉS

PREPARATION : ARM—

COUNT &
1 ... 2

CLOSE
BEHIND

D

1 2 3

GRANDS BATTEMENTS EN CROIX

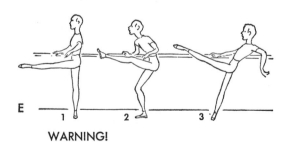

E

1 2 3

WARNING!

C. *Battements tendus* can also be performed with a *demi-plié* in the closed positions.

D. *Grands battements* ("big beatings"). The instructions for *battements tendus* also apply to *grands battements*, which are the throwing up of a straight leg, beginning and ending with a *tendu* as sketched. They are performed *en croix*, and can be done four times in each direction to begin with, and eight times as the pupil progresses. The purpose is to promote a general circulation of blood through the legs and to loosen the hip joints. Don't try to throw your leg too high at first or you will probably achieve the positions shown in Fig. E, 2 and 3. Keep the leg lower, but make sure it is properly turned out. *Battements tendus* are usually performed to crisp 4/4 time, *en croix* 4 times with each leg (*i.e.*, facing each way). 4/4 time also goes for *grands battements*, but played a little slower than for the *tendus*.

E. Fig. 1 shows a young man who has that "trained" look, and this is because he has a sense of balance in more ways than one. He knows that to control his *grands battements* is more important than untidy "high kicks." Moreover, of the three students shown he is the only one who could repeat the movement without the aid of the *barre*; and it must be remembered that dancers can't take the *barre* onto the stage with them . . .

Don't make the silly mistakes of Figs. 2 and 3, who both seem to think they are managing better than Fig. 1 because (somehow) they have got their legs a little higher.

iii. RONDS DE JAMBE, *à terre* and *en l'air; BATTE-MENTS FRAPPÉS and SUR LE COU DE PIED*

A. *Ronds de jambe à terre* ("rounds with the leg on the ground") *en dehors* (outwards) and *en dedans* (inwards) are exercises to loosen the hip joint. They are always done outwards first (Figs. A, 5 and 8). Performed to a slow 3/4 time, the first beat of the bar always finds the heels together in 1st position. The working leg should move smoothly and continuously when the exercise has been learned, but a good method for the very beginning is to do the "round" in four stages, *i.e.* in slow motion, using a whole bar for each movement. E.g., for *en dehors:* at the end of the preparation the working leg is in 2nd position *pointe tendue* (point stretched) as in Fig. A 4. The toes then proceed to "draw the round" by passing first to the 4th position behind, then through first position (both heels down) as in Fig. 5, dotted line; then *pointe tendue* to the 4th in front, then to the 2nd once more, and so on. At no time does the toe of the working leg leave the ground. The hip of the supporting leg should be well lifted —don't "sit" on it. For *en dedans,* reverse the directions for *en dehors;* the preparation is the same. Do 8 *ronds de jambe* each way with each leg.

B. *Battements frappés* ("knocked beats") are for strengthening and developing the instep, and also serve to increase the ultimate elevation of the student. When the heel of the working leg is placed on either side of the ankle of the supporting leg (B, 2 and 4) the foot should be relaxed as shown. As in Figs. 3 and 5, the working foot extends sharply to the 2nd position, hitting the floor as it goes (hence the "knock"), and when thus extended (Fig. 3) the toe should not be more than 2 inches off the ground. Exercise: 16 counts with each leg.

1 - 4   Preparation for RONDS DE JAMBE à terre en dehors

A

RONDS DE JAMBE À TERRE

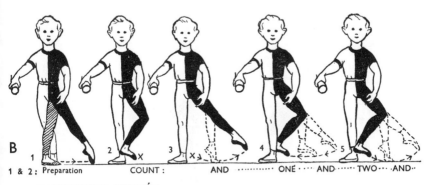

B

1 & 2 : Preparation   COUNT :   AND ·············· ONE ···· AND ······· TWO ··· AND··

BATTEMENTS FRAPPÉS

C, 2–4: *battements sur le cou de pied* ("beats on the neck of the foot"). This exercise is a preparation for future *batterie* (part of advanced steps such as *brisés* and *entrechâts* (see pages 78–79). At first this movement should be practised very slowly with equal accent both when the feet are together and apart; then double time; gradually increasing the speed as the pupil becomes more adept. Practise for 32 counts with each leg, and increase after the first few months. C5: *battements sur le cou de pied sur la demi-pointe* ("on half point"). This movement is exactly the same as the previous one, but the instep of the working foot is fully stretched, as sketch, and the supporting foot on half point throughout. Don't allow the body to sway and wobble, and don't attempt this exercise until you have mastered the previous one. 16 counts for each leg.

D. *Ronds de jambe en l'air* ("in the air"). For flexibility of the knee joint and to aid the turn-out of the thigh, which should be held motionless and well back during the exercise. Figs. 2, 3, and 4 constitute the preparation, before music begins; this should be a moderate waltz tempo. Each "round" is accompanied by one bar of music, the first beat of which always finds the working leg extended *à la seconde*, the third when it is touching the calf of the supporting leg. Study the plans of all *ronds de jambe* carefully (A, 7 and 8, on the preceding page, and D, 6, opposite); neither should be complete circles. Opposite, Fig. 4 shows *en dedans*, 5 *en dehors*.

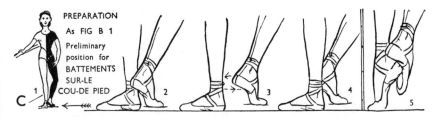

PREPARATION
As FIG B 1
Preliminary
position for
BATTEMENTS
SUR-LE
COU-DE-PIED

BATTEMENTS SUR LE COU-DE-PIED

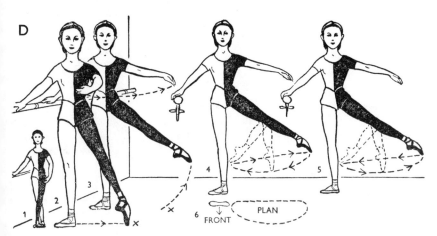

PLAN

FRONT

RONDS DE JAMBE EN L'AIR

DÉVELOPPÉS À LA BARRE (EN CROIX)

(Preliminary method)

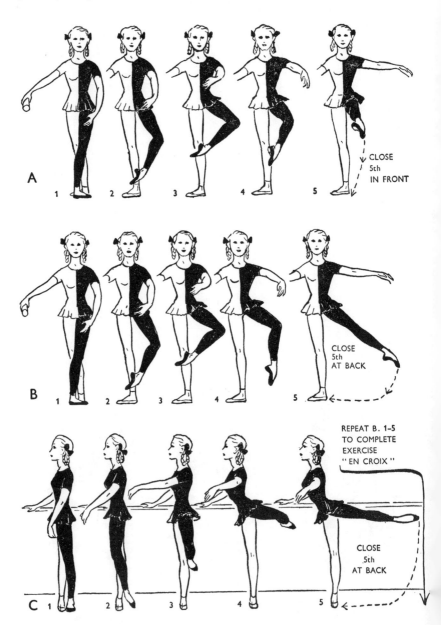

CLOSE
5th
IN FRONT

A 1 2 3 4 5

CLOSE
5th
AT BACK

B 1 2 3 4 5

REPEAT B. 1–5
TO COMPLETE
EXERCISE
" EN CROIX "

CLOSE
5th
AT BACK

C 1 2 3 4 5

iv. DÉVELOPPÉS; BATTEMENTS EN CLÔCHE

From the verb *développer*, to develop or unfold, *développés* are an exercise featuring control of the legs, to aid the execution of *adage*, which will be found farther on under *Centre Practice*; they are performed to music of slow 3/4 time. Sequence A: Fig. 1, the preliminary position; Fig. 2–B1, inclusive, the actual unfolding movement known as a *développé*. They are done *en croix* here—take four bars of music for each one. A good method for the beginner, to avoid undue strain, is to do one sequence *en croix* with one leg, turn and repeat with the other, and so on. It should be borne in mind that full control of the legs takes many years to accomplish, so don't try to raise the thigh above the level of the hip, as this is in the province of the more advanced student (see D). A low but well-placed leg is more desirable than one placed very high but turned in and accompanied by contortions by the rest of the body, and too much pressure on the *barre*.

Notice that in sequence C, Fig. 4, the leg is passing through the position known as *attitude* (see p. 50). Note also that only in a *développé* to the back is the body allowed to tilt slightly forward. E. *Battements en clôche* ("beatings like the swing of a bell"). This movement is to produce freedom of the hip socket and for circulation. The preparation is with the working leg *pointe tendue* at the back, the first movement forward. Take care that both legs are perfectly straight throughout. It is done to a quick 3/4 or slow 6/8 rhythm; if 3/4 time is used, continue swinging the leg back and front until 16 bars have elapsed, or 8 bars of 6/8, using three beats to swing the leg to the front, three to the back.

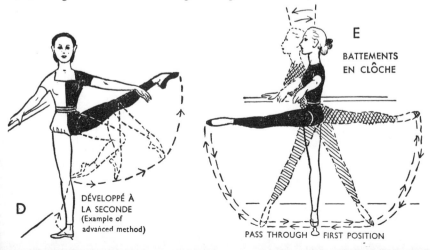

E
BATTEMENTS
EN CLÔCHE

D

DÉVELOPPÉ À
LA SECONDE
(Example of
advanced method)

PASS THROUGH FIRST POSITION

v. RELEVÉS *from two feet on to one*

From the verb *relever*, to rise. *Relevés* are very much used in ballet by both male and female students. Here they serve to strengthen the arch of the supporting foot when on *demi-pointe*, which makes it an important exercise for general balance. It also accustoms the dancer to pull up the knee and leg muscles after the comparative relaxation of the *demi-plié* —which stands the dancer in good stead when in actual movement. It is also a preparation for *pointe*-work. Sketches A, 2–5, a *relevé devant* (in front); 6–7, *relevé derrière* (at the back); 8–9, *relevé passé en arrière* (passed to the back), raising the front foot sharply to the front of the supporting knee, closing 5th at the back; 10–11, *relevé passé en avant* (passed to the front) raising the back foot quickly to the back, side, and front of the supporting knee before closing 5th in front. *Note.*—The term *relevé* really relates to the *supporting foot*, which rises sharply to the *demi-pointe* by means of a slight spring, in the manner shown by the first sketch on this page. After each *relevé*, both feet return to their original positions simultaneously, again with a slight spring.

vi. COUPÉS *à la barre*

Coupés (from *couper*, to cut) are so called because one foot appears to be cutting the ground away from the other. They are usually employed in conjunction with other steps, such as *ballonnés, fouettés*, etc., which the student would learn in more advanced grades. For typical use of *coupés* see pp. 75 and 76.

On right, Figs. B, 1–4 show a *coupé dessous* (under), which for the purpose of an exercise would be followed immediately by a *coupé dessus* (over) as shown by Figs. 5–7.

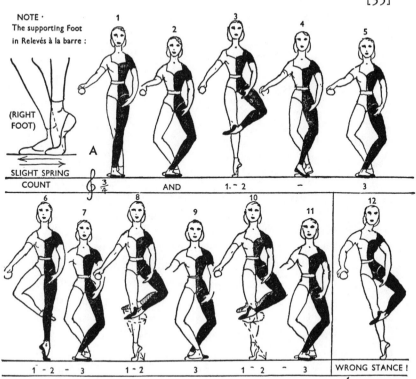

NOTE ·
The supporting Foot
in Relevés à la barre :

(RIGHT FOOT)

SLIGHT SPRING

A

| COUNT | $\frac{3}{4}$ | AND | 1. - 2 | - | 3 |

| 1 - 2 - 3 | 1 - 2 | 3 | 1 - 2 - 3 | WRONG STANCE ! |

RELEVES

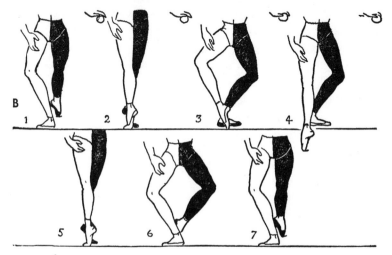

B

COUPÉS

IV. BEGINNER'S CLASS:
SECOND HALF

i. *PRELIMINARY NOTES ON CENTRE PRACTICE*

At the end of the preceding work at the *barre*, which should take the average student about half an hour, the body should be sufficiently "warmed up" to start work without the aid of the *barre*; with the circulation running properly one can feel and control the muscles with comparative ease.

For the first two months, in order that the student may become thoroughly acquainted with those exercises at the *barre*, the latter should be repeated in the centre of the room without the aid of the *barre* (but beginners should except *battements sur le cou de pied, sur la demi-pointe* and *battements en clôche*). The arm which until now rested on the *barre* should make exactly the same movements as the working arm.

After two months, the student may begin to combine these *barre* exercises in various ways; *e.g.*, 8 counts of *battements frappés* followed by 8 counts of *battements sur le cou de pied* with the same foot, the same the other side, etc. After this, the *barre* exercises may be used in conjunction with other movements of the arms and body, in the same way that *battements tendus* and *grands battements* are used with the *Eight Directions of the Body* on pp. 42–43.

As times goes on and the student becomes thoroughly familiar with the *barre* work, some of the repetition in the centre may be omitted, thus leaving more time for practising *adage*, *allégro*, and other centre practice.

ii. THE FIVE BASIC POSITIONS OF THE ARMS
(*see sketches overleaf*)

To show the basic positions of the arms, the Cecchetti system has been adopted. These positions remain more or less the same as taught by other methods, but the order may differ. The student should memorise these positions immediately, because, like the five positions of the feet, dancing cannot take place without them.

Attention is drawn to the 1st position, in which the tip of the middle finger of each hand should lightly touch the sides of the thighs; and to the 5th position *en bas*, in which the sides of the little fingers should be allowed to touch the front of the thighs.

In all these positions the shoulders should be kept *down*, particularly in 5th *en haut* when it is very easy to hunch them. The elbows should never be allowed to cave in and should always be supported (which will make them ache, but never mind). The wrist should also be supported in all positions and never be allowed to flap either up or down. The fingers are held closely together with the thumb pulled slightly towards the palm of the hand. A soft, clear line should be practised from shoulder to fingertips, controlled but never strained in appearance; and all disagreeable angles like "broken" wrists, pointed elbows, and crooked little fingers avoided with very great care.

DONT DO THIS!
AGONIZED EXPRESSION →
HUNCHED SHOULDER
DROPPED WRIST
AFFECTED FINGERS
CAVED-IN ELBOW

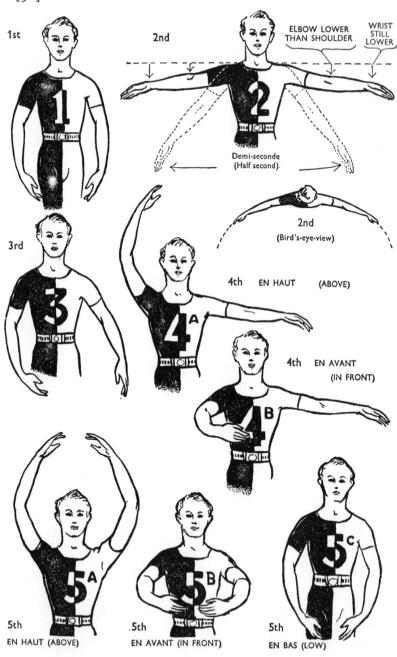

[38]

1st

2nd — ELBOW LOWER THAN SHOULDER — WRIST STILL LOWER

Demi-seconde (Half second).

2nd (Bird's-eye-view)

3rd

4th   EN HAUT   (ABOVE)

4th   EN AVANT (IN FRONT)

5th EN HAUT (ABOVE)

.5th EN AVANT (IN FRONT)

5th EN BAS (LOW)

V. CENTRE PRACTICE

(EXERCISES AU MILIEU)

i. *EXERCISES IN PORT DE BRAS* (*Carriage of the Arms*)

Generally speaking, the word "expression" is applied to the face alone; but the exercises in *port de bras* given here are a first study in *the expressive use of the arms*. Moreover, the ballet dancer is not confined to the expression of anger, pleasure, fear, etc., but the whole body is constantly called upon to interpret many shades of poetic emotion to accompany the various kinds of music. For showing these delicate nuances, the most expressive part of the body, next to the face, is the arms.

In the four exercises illustrated (sequence A below, B, C, and D overleaf), the body faces a *croisée* direction (see position termed *croisée devant* on p. 42). A slow ¾ time music should be used; 4 bars should accompany each sequence as sketched, and each sequence should be performed four times facing the two opposite corners of the room. The arms and head should move together smoothly and continuously, avoiding jerkiness and pauses. Here is the first opportunity of applying in centre practice all you have learned at the *barre* concerning posture—knees pulled up, body straight and slim—together with all you have been told about the use of the arms; shoulders down, rounded and supported elbows, and simple hands.

Pay careful attention to the sketches and note whether the head is inclined, turned, raised, or lowered.

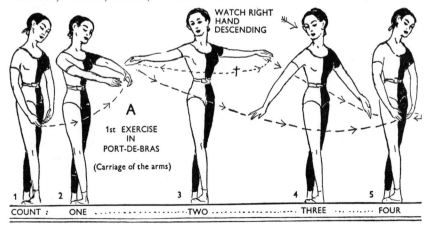

WATCH RIGHT HAND DESCENDING

A

1st EXERCISE IN PORT-DE-BRAS

(Carriage of the arms)

1　2　3　4　5

COUNT : ONE · · · · · · · · · · · · · · TWO · · · · · · · · · · · · · · THREE · · · · · · · · FOUR

2nd EXERCISE IN PORT-DE-BRAS

5 ARMS AS EN ARABESQUE

RIGHT ARM PASSES THROUGH 1st POSITION

B COUNT—preparation

ONE ... AND ... TWO ... THREE ... FOUR

3rd EXERCISE

2 & 3 ARMS IN FIFTH POSITION EN HAUT

C COUNT AND ONE TWO THREE AND FOUR

4th EXERCISE

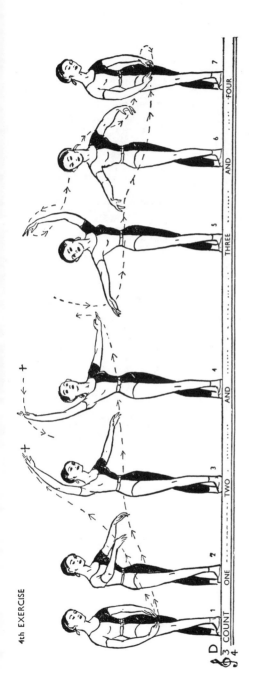

Port de bras—continued: 2nd, 3rd, and 4th exercises

In relation to the established positions of the arms: in the second exercise (seq. B) the arms start in 5th *en bas* (B1); right arm brushes through 1st position into an *arabesque* position (see p. 49, left arm of Sketch B); at the same time the left arm passes through 5th *en avant* into a variation of the position known as *attitude* (B2). From there, both arms (travelling different ways) pass into 2nd (B3), into *arabesque* (B5), and to 5th *en bas* again (B6) and so on.

These exercises are more difficult than they appear at first glance, as they feature independent control of the arms at the same time. *E.g.*, B1–2: it is obvious that the left arm has a considerable distance to travel, the right arm a short distance; but both arms must reach Sketch 2 at the same moment, neither of them passing en route. Don't be discouraged if it is difficult at first; dancers take years to perfect their arms. Just take a look at any action photograph to see proof of this.

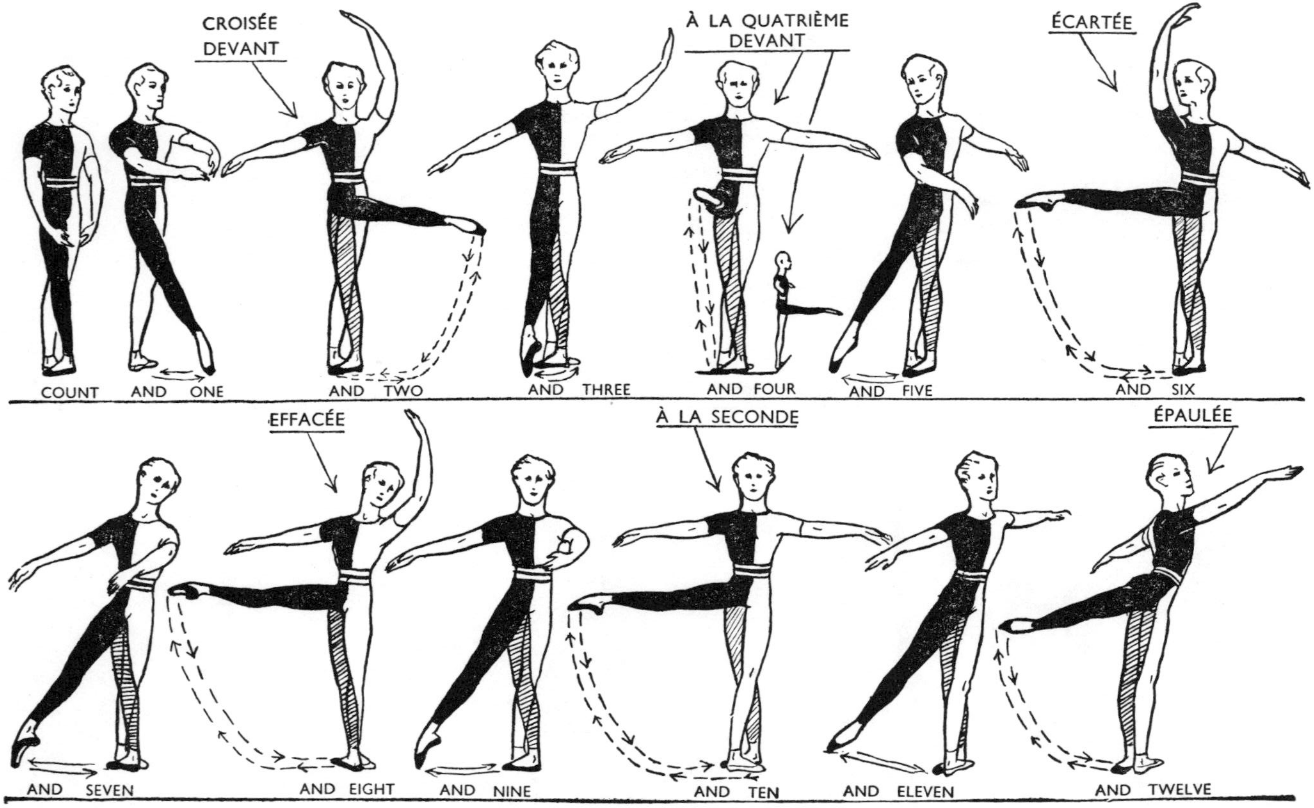

CROISÉE DEVANT

À LA QUATRIÈME DEVANT

ÉCARTÉE

COUNT AND ONE

AND TWO

AND THREE

AND FOUR

AND FIVE

AND SIX

EFFACÉE

À LA SECONDE

ÉPAULÉE

AND SEVEN

AND EIGHT

AND NINE

AND TEN

AND ELEVEN

AND TWELVE

À LA QUATRIÈME DERRIÈRE

CROISÉE DERRIÈRE

Repeat entire exercise with other leg, etc.

AND THIRTEEN   AND FOURTEEN   AND FIFTEEN   AND SIXTEEN   AND ONE   AND TWO   etc.

ii. THE EIGHT DIRECTIONS OF THE BODY
as an exercise with battements tendus and grands battements

The eight directions of the body are as follows:

1. *Croisée devant* (crossed front).
2. *À la quatrième devant* (to the fourth front).
3. *Écartée* (separated, or thrown wide apart).
4. *Effacée* (shaded).
5. *À la seconde* (to the second).
6. *Épaulée* (shouldered).
7. *À la quatrième derrière* (to the fourth back).
8. *Croisée derrière* (crossed back).

Like the five positions of the feet and arms, the eight directions of the body govern many of the movements in dancing. They should therefore be memorised by the student as quickly as possible. These sketches show the eight directions linked by *battements tendus*, with a *grand battement* performed in each of the main postures. *The legs and body change direction at the same time that the battement tendu is being performed.* As in the preceding exercises in *port de bras*, the arms should move smoothly and continuously, avoiding jerkiness.

A

B

C

D

ABCD = four ¼ turns as Preliminary Exercise for Pirouettes en dehors

iii. PIROUETTES

From the French verb *pirouetter*, "to whirl," in ballet a *pirouette* denotes spinning on one leg. Here we have chosen a *pirouette en dehors* because this is usual for the beginner, but there are many other kinds.

On the stage, *pirouettes* stand out as brilliant facets in both the ballerina's and the male dancer's performance. It should be emphasized at once that the brilliant effect is due not only to the number of *pirouettes* performed, but to the manner in which they are executed—which should be extremely neat and in exact timing with the music.

Figs. A, B, C, and D: exercise for *pirouettes en dehors* in quarter turns. Seq. A: stand facing front, feet 5th position with left foot front. With the front or working foot execute *tendu* to the side, taking the arms to 2nd position. Working foot now traces a *demi rond de jambe en dehors*, ending in 4th *croisée* with a *demi-plié*. At the same time the left arm moves forward to 5th *en avant*. Bring the arms sharply down to 5th *en bas*, *relevé* raising the working foot in front, at the same time making a quarter turn towards raised foot. Then close both feet together with a slight spring into *demi-plié*, working foot in front (see *relevés* on p. 35), opening the arms slightly forward as sketch. This completes first quarter turn. Follow the same instructions for seqs. B, C, and D, as illustrated; then put other foot in front and repeat the other way.

Seq. E illustrates a single complete *pirouette*. The rules are the same as for the quarter turns, except that the use of the head comes into play, in order to prevent giddiness, to gain impetus, and to give a brilliant effect. Broadly speaking, the idea is to focus the eyes on a spot directly in front, to look at it as long as possible whilst the body is turning, then to bring the head sharply around to the front again before the body has finished turning.

After practising the quarter turns, and before attempting the complete *pirouette*, *half* turns should be practised applying the same head principles as in E.

For all the above exercises, music should be 4/4 time; the *tendu* is done to the first beat, *demi-plié* in fourth to the second beat, *relevé* to the third beat, closing of the feet to the fourth beat in the bar.

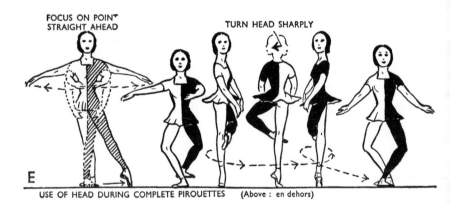

FOCUS ON POINT STRAIGHT AHEAD

TURN HEAD SHARPLY

E

USE OF HEAD DURING COMPLETE PIROUETTES   (Above : en dehors)

From the finale
"Les Sylphides"—
a free
rendering of
3rd arabesque
with
temps levé.

iv. FIRST ARABESQUES

An *arabesque* is a beautiful pose which has now become a household word and hardly needs introduction to the general reader. From the point of view of execution, however, it is not such a simple matter.

The first step towards a good *arabesque* is to dispense completely with the idea that the essence of this pose is to stand on one leg and then kick the back one as high as possible. The quality of an *arabesque* will improve only as the quality of your technique improves, and a good *arabesque* will be the reward of the student who has worked hard at the rather boring aspects of ballet technique at the *barre*: general posture, which includes well-controlled feet, pulled-up knee muscles, and straight body. If the student hasn't bothered to attend to these important details and has been standing as the girls on p. 21, A1 and 2, the result will be ungainly poses such as H and I opposite, or worse, a nasty fall. The correct execution of *grands battements* at the back (p. 26, D3) is very important, with the upper part of the body tilted slightly forward, the chest raised, and the supporting leg straight. An *arabesque* is a pose of quality rather than an acrobatic feat (see F)—this is why it is in an *arabesque* that the characters of various students show most strongly; whether they are lazy, flashy, conceited, or have good taste.

There are many different kinds of *arabesques*, but the *first arabesque*, as shown, is the most familiar of all and also the one which is learned first by the beginner. Sequence A shows a *first arabesque* preceded by a *chassé* from a *demi-plié* in the 5th position. (*Chasser*, lit. "to chase.") In this case: slide the front foot forward until the weight of the body is distributed equally between both legs; straighten both knees, at the same time transferring the weight of the body on to the front leg, stretching the back foot into *pointe tendue* and using the arms as shown (B); this pose is known as *first arabesque à terre* (on the ground). Slowly raise the back leg a few inches from the ground without moving the body. When you feel you have lifted your leg in this way as high as physically possible, allow the body to tilt slightly forward, raising the back leg at the same time (C). If you allow the body to tilt forward without raising your leg you will achieve H, and unless you keep your demeanour simple—see G. After a few months' study you may tilt the body further and attempt an *arabesque allongée* (lengthened, D). Sketch E shows a *penchée* (pitched) position as the final aspect of the *first arabesque*, but this pose should not be attempted by first year students.

CHASSÉ À LA QUATRIÈME EN AVANT

A 1   2   3

B   ← 1st ARABESQUE (À TERRE)

C   1st ARABESQUE

1st ARABESQUE. ALLONGÉE

D

1st ARABESQUE. PENCHÉE

E

F

H

WARNINGS

G

I

CHASSÉ
À LA
QUATRIÈME
EN AVANT

1
2
3

ATTITUDE
CROISÉE À TERRE

BIRD'S EYE
VIEW OF
ATTITUDE
CROISÉE

ATTITUDE
CROISÉE

BODY TURNED
TO LEFT FRONT
CORNER OF
STAGE

v. ATTITUDES, EFFACÉE AND CROISÉE

The pose known as attitude is based on a famous figure of Mercury by Gian Bologna (or Jean de Bologne). It has much in common with the *arabesque* (see previous page)

HUNCHED SHOULDERS

DROPPED WRIST

JUTTING ELBOW

ARM TOO HIGH

SITTING ON HIP

BENT KNEE

WORKING LEG
AND SUPPORTING LEG
BOTH TURNED IN

DON'T DO THIS!

CHASSÉ
À LA
QUATRIÈME
EN AVANT

ATTITUDE EFFACÉE
À TERRE

BODY TURNED
TO RIGHT FRONT
CORNER OF STAGE

ATTITUDE EFFACÉE

as it is also a beautiful pose in itself, and both are much used in the course of actual dance movement—jumps and turns are performed *en attitude* and *en arabesque*, and both figure largely in the execution of *adage*. Among the most lovely and effective movements in ballet are turns in *attitude*, but these are for the more advanced student.

Attitude effacée (above): for a preparation, stand facing an *effacée* direction (see p. 42), right foot front, as Fig. 1. Execute a *chassé* as described on the previous page (Figs. 2 and 3) into *attitude à terre*, with the weight of the body well over the front foot. Note the inclination of the head towards the raised arm. Raise the back leg *en l'air* by *lifting the thigh*, into *attitude effacé*, as sketch. In all *attitudes* the knee should be higher from the ground than the foot. See p. 32, Fig. C4, at the *barre*. To perform *attitude croisée*, follow the sketches using the same method as for *attitude effacée*.

VI. CENTRE PRACTICE (CONTINUED):

ADAGE

CHASSÉ À LA QUATRIÈME EN AVANT

ATTITUDE CROISÉE A TERRE

ATTITUDE CROISÉE EN L'AIR

VALSE, OP 69, NO 1 *CHOPIN*

FOUR

pas de bourrée dessous

OF   HEEL

ADAGE i. *EXERCISES IN ADAGE—AN EXAMPLE*

PIROUETTE
EN
DEHORS

REPEAT
EXERCISE
ON
OTHER
SIDE

24   25   26   27   28   29

ii. NOTES ON ADAGE

Adage is the French version of *ad agio*, an Italian term largely used in music, which literally translated means "at leisure." In ballet this indicates a slow dance in which all parts of the body are used simultaneously to give a harmonious effect; the onlooker may find such an exercise very soothing to watch, but it is anything but "leisurely" for the dancer.

When the teacher says: "Let us do some *adage*," this means that several steps are to be combined together to make a slow poetic dance. Usually, a different combination is given each time, and this gives the student practice at picking up and memorising sequences of steps quickly, and mastering the various difficulties of execution which usually occur when passing from one step to another. Here is another occasion when the character and musical sense of the student first begin to take shape.

An example of an elementary *adage* is given here, starting on p. 52 and concluding above. Taking the movements one by one, they are as follows:

A *chassé* (Figs. 1, 2, 3):

attitudes croisée (5), *en face* (facing) (6), and *effacée* (7):

into—*arabesque fondue allongée* with the arms in *attitude*
("*fondue*" from *fondre*, "to sink," signifying a bend on
one leg with the other raised);

pas de bourrée dessus (see p. 62, C) (9–10–11);

developpé into *second arabesque* (13–14–15) (*second arabesque* is the same as *first arabesque* but with the other
leg raised); and so into

arabesque fondue allongé (21);

pas de bourrée dessous into 4th position of the feet(22–23–24);

pirouette en dedans (25–28).

When a pivot is made on one leg (as in Figs. 5–6–7, and
later in Figs. 16–20), the movement is termed a *promenade*.

The music chosen for this little *adage* is the valse op. 69 by
Chopin, and it has been arranged here so that the bars coincide
with the dancer's movements in order that some idea of accompaniment can be obtained. Note also that the music is
headed *con espressione*, "with expression," which is the
kind of music you should always choose for *adage*. Some of
Chopin's *Nocturnes* are also highly suitable.

Until this point, the music accompanying the exercises has
been indicated merely as 6/8, 4/4, etc., because its main purpose has been to provide a rhythmic accompaniment for the
steps. To arrange an *adage* to music is a far more subtle matter,
and a technical knowledge of music, as well as a natural musical sense, is of the greatest possible value to ballet teachers,
students, and critics.

VII. CENTRE PRACTICE

(CONTINUED)

Allégro and Steps of Elevation

i. GENERAL OBSERVATIONS

Musically, the term *allégro* indicates "quick and lively." A great many steps in ballet come under this heading. The gliding movements called *glissades*, the brilliant and intricate *pas de bourrées*, the little jumps called *sautés*, the long smooth leaps known as *grands jetés*, are a few examples. Then there is the difference between steps of the same name when performed in different ways; for example, *échappés sautés* (p. 65) are a large movement compared with the pizzicato effect of *échappés relevés sur les pointes* (p. 75).

Steps of *allégro* are NEVER attempted till the body is perfectly "warmed up." A large proportion of accidents are due to failure to note this classic regulation.

In the course of the graceful *arabesques* and *attitudes* and the slow elegance of *adage* as recently described, a certain type of dancer [1] will have shown to advantage—the loose-limbed, supple individual with high insteps. With the introduction of *pas d'allégro*, however, the opposite type will score; the stockier, broader person who usually has strong, rather flat feet and clearly defined muscles. Briefly, the first type tends towards a knock-knee and usually has an inborn facility for slow, graceful movement; the second has a tendency towards bandiness and at the same time a natural dexterity in sharp, brilliant movement, an excellent sense of timing, and good elevation. Both these physical defects can be greatly minimised (and in many cases, cured) by paying much attention to exer-

[1] See "Physical Aspects," *The Ballet-Lover's Companion*, p. 20.

cises at the *barre* and to basic deportment; and each type should work particularly hard at those steps which are the hardest for him or her to master.

To return to the second, less graceful type; there is a well-known dancer who conforms to these proportions, and of him a spectator was heard to say: "You only notice his face when he is doing slow movements, and he must be quite heavy; but when he moves fast—whew! he flashes about like a shrimp in a puddle!"

In steps of *allégro* it is very important to pay heed to neatness and vitality of expression, and control of the arms is much more difficult than you would think, too. A small movement looks highly ridiculous if accompanied by flapping arms. Also, don't make the mistake of thinking that because the steps are small, they are insignificant. Remember that shrimp! Small steps can, and should, flash like quicksilver.

These strongly made types often experience difficulty at first with the small, neat but important steps. Just as often, however, they are gifted with a remarkable power of elevation, which can easily be perceived in the classroom, where they can be seen soaring above the heads of their fellows. Now, it is more usual to see a beginner jumping as high as this than a finished performer. But the uncontrolled leaper will lose his power of elevation, due to physical injuries—unless he is willing to study the *science* of leaping in ballet.

Although a great elevation can be a tremendous asset, in its early stages it is an equally tremendous danger. Jumping in ballet is not a sport, and height is by no means the sole object. Imagine a young man high in the air, having got up there by some means or other, bunched up like a hurdler, and landing with a crash on his heels. We do not see leaps executed in this manner on the stage because such a performer could never get a job as a ballet artist, however high he could leap, and also because if he jumped in this manner continuously his natural elevation would soon be a thing of the past.

Controlling and increasing one's elevation is a lengthy subject on its own. Here, however, we must confine ourselves to the main essentials which govern the first steps of elevation in ballet, which will repay the most careful study.

(1) *A good preparation ensures a good jump.* Whether the spring comes from both feet, as in *échappés sautés changés* on p. 65, or from one foot, as sketched in *jetés derrières* on p. 67, a good "bend" of the knees is essential with the heels firmly on the ground. (Try a jump without bending the knees and see what happens!) Without this bending of the knees, the heels—which are responsible for all elevation—cannot give you a good push upwards.

(2) Once in the air, it is essential that the knees and feet are as straight—*i.e.,* as fully stretched—as possible; not only for appearances' sake, but to ensure a soft, correct, *and safe* landing.

(3) Taking the landing from a jump in slow motion; the toes should be the first to touch the ground, and passing rapidly through the intermediate foot positions (see p. 21, Figs. C3, 2, and 1) the heels should follow, the movement being completed with a *demi-plié* of the knees.

A jump which is not followed by a *plié* is liable to break your knees for you—no less. If you do bend your knees on landing, but insufficiently, you will make a noise like a house falling down, which is unæsthetic, to say the least.

Failure to bring the heels down to the ground after each step of elevation tends to thicken the Achilles tendon. Being a very common fault amongst ballet dancers, it has given rise to the popular belief that the study of ballet leads to thick ankles. *Improperly performed,* it does.

"IMPROPERLY PERFORMED—"

ii. SAUTÉ, CHANGEMENT, AND GLISSADES (*illustrated on pp.* 60 *and* 61)

1. *Sauté* is from *sauter*, "to jump." It is advisable to execute sixteen of these little jumps continuously to warm and strengthen the feet as a prelude to steps of *allégro*. They are performed in the 1st position of the feet.

2. *Changement*, from *changer*, "to change," so called because the feet change position in mid-air, *on the way down* each time. Perform sixteen. In these two exercises do not tilt the body either backwards or forwards.

3. *Glissade*, from *glisser*, "to slide." When following the sketches be careful not to give a jerky effect; treat the five figures in each sequence as one complete movement. At first the *glissades* should be practised slowly and smoothly to a 3/4 time, with the last figure of each sequence representing the first beat of the bar. Gradually increase the speed until the movement becomes sharp and neat. Carefully memorise the different placing of the feet and the special head movement which goes with each.

4. An example of *glissades* as they may be used one after another to make a little exercise.

N.B.—*Derrière* denotes "behind"; *devant*, "in front"; *dessus*, "over"; *dessous*, "under"; *en avant*, "coming forwards" *en arrière*, "going backwards."

ALLEGRO—SEE PAGE 59 FOR EXPLANATION

1 SAUTÉ **2 CHANGEMENT**

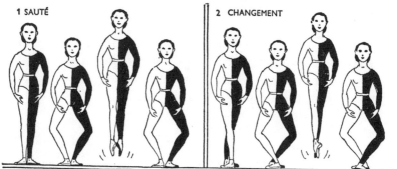

3 (i) GLISSADE DERRIÈRE

3 (ii) GLISSADE DEVANT

3 (iii) GLISSADE DESSUS

3 (iv) GLISSADE DESSOUS

3 (v) GLISSADE EN AVANT

SLIDE FORWARD

3 (vi) GLISSADE EN ARRIÈRE

SLIDE BACKWARDS

4   3 GLISSADES (DERRIÈRE) WITH CHANGEMENTS AS AN EXERCISE

(NOTE USE OF ARMS)

1 (A) PAS DE BOURRÉE DERRIÈRE

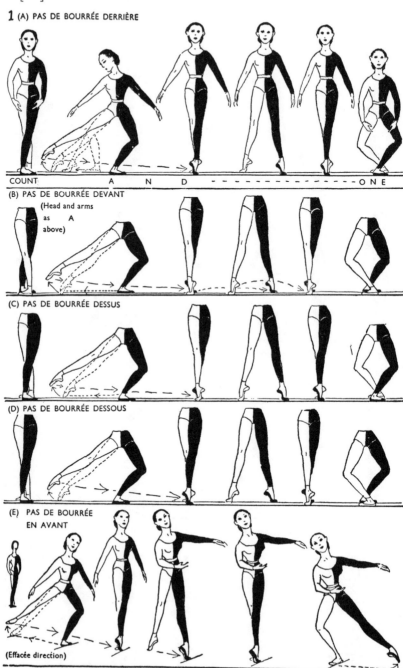

COUNT	A	N	D	- - - - - - - - - - - - - - - - O N E

(B) PAS DE BOURRÉE DEVANT

(Head and arms
as   A
above)

(C) PAS DE BOURRÉE DESSUS

(D) PAS DE BOURRÉE DESSOUS

(E) PAS DE BOURRÉE
    EN AVANT

(Effacée direction)

(F) PAS DE BOURRÉE
EN ARRIÈRE

iii. *PAS DE BOURRÉES*

Musically speaking, a *bourrée* denotes a dance in 2/4 time starting with an up-beat. In ballet there are countless varieties of *bourrées;* they are not only used as steps by themselves but are used to move from one position to another; when a dancer crosses the stage with tiny twinkling steps *sur les pointes*, this is a species of *bourrée*. The examples given here are the first ones you will learn in class.

Study the sketches carefully. Note that in sequences E and F the body on both occasions faces an *effacée* direction. *Pas de bourrées en avant* and *en arrière* are often performed together as an exercise going forwards and backwards, so the last sketch in each sequence shows the figure ready to move in the opposite direction. For a single example of each of these two steps, close the foot in 5th position, as in the previous *pas de bourrées*, Figs. A–D.

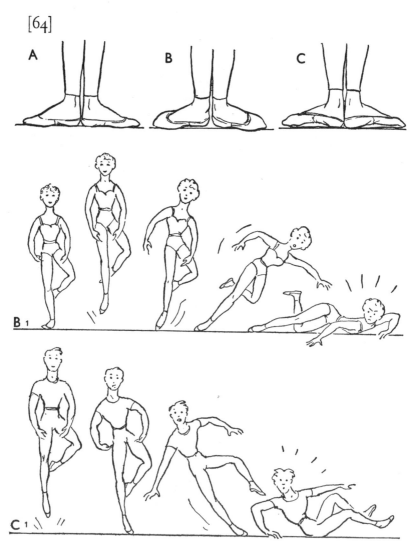

iv. WARNINGS!

If you have not been paying attention to the rules of deportment given on p. 21 at the *barre* and at all times during your practice, here are just two examples of what may happen when you try to jump. A, well-placed feet and ankles. B, the ankles roll over forwards. B1, the result in an attempted *temps levé*. C, the ankles roll outwards or backwards. C1, the result.

A ÉCHAPPÉS SAUTÉS CHANGÉS

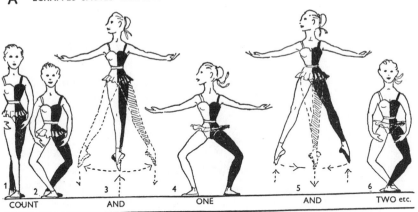

| 1 | 2 | 3 | 4 | 5 | 6 |
| COUNT | | AND | ONE | AND | TWO etc. |

v. A. ÉCHAPPÉS SAUTÉS CHANGÉS (from *échapper*, "to escape")

Perform four times (from Figs. 2–10), jumping as high as possible with a big *demi-plié*. Get your breath, then repeat in a smaller, quicker manner.

B. and C. JETÉS DERRIÈRES AND DEVANTS (from *jeter*, "to throw")

There are many different kinds of *jetés*, but these are the first you will learn. It is the first time that you will have to spring from one leg and land on the other. You must not travel sideways, but *jetés derrières* travel forward the width of one of your feet with each step, *jetés devants* backwards. The best way to try them is in a small way at first, eight *derrière* and then eight *devant* with alternate feet. Repeat the exercise more slowly and with higher elevation as you progress. The working foot brushes the ground and this is what pushes you upwards. Make sure that for a second both the legs are straight in the air.

D. JETÉS DERRIÈRES

Arranged as an exercise with *temps levés* (lit. "lifted" steps, denoting hops).

E. COUPÉS SAUTÉS

A variety of the *coupés* at the barre, here used with a small jump as a step of *allégro*.

E COUPÉS SAUTÉES

Transfer the weight from one foot to the other so that the lifted foot rises sharply and the landing foot falls softly (the latter is the foot that makes the "cut"). For the correct use of the foot in landing, see notes on p. 58, paragraph 3. Do 16 *coupés*, right foot front, and repeat with left foot front.

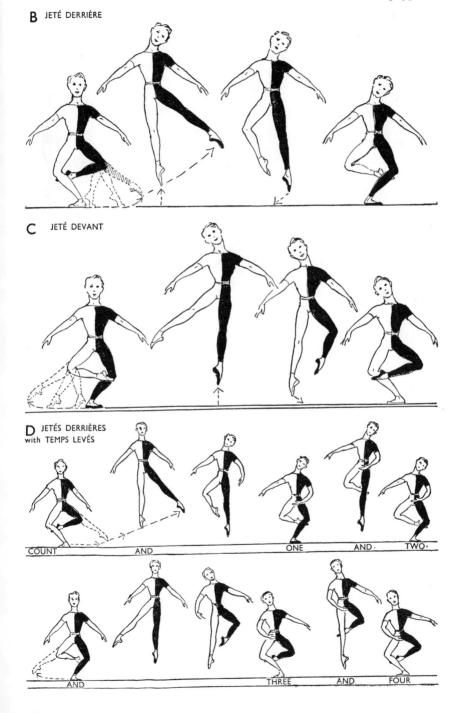

B JETÉ DERRIÈRE

C JETÉ DEVANT

D JETÉS DERRIÈRES
with TEMPS LEVÉS

COUNT   AND   ONE   AND ·   TWO ·

AND   THREE   AND   FOUR

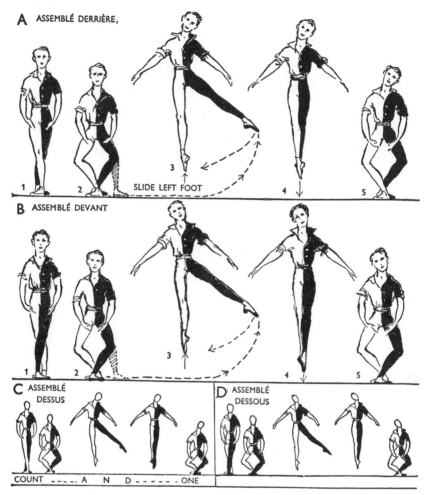

A ASSEMBLÉ DERRIÈRE,

1 2 3 SLIDE LEFT FOOT 4 5

B ASSEMBLÉ DEVANT

1 2 3 4 5

C ASSEMBLÉ DESSUS

D ASSEMBLÉ DESSOUS

COUNT ..... A   N   D ..... ONE

vi. ASSEMBLÉS (from *assembler,* "to put together"): SOUBRESAUT

In this case assembling the feet in the air, before landing. In the sequences Fig. 4 is the one where the most common mistake occurs. You *must* assemble your feet before landing. Again, as in *jetés,* you gain impetus for your jump by

brushing the working foot along the ground before taking off.
It takes quite a while to learn this movement, but when
learned, it will be possible to try the little exercise shown
above, composed of *glissades*, *assemblés*, and a *soubresaut* ("a
jump")—a straight jump with the feet in 5th position. Pay
special attention to the use of the head—there are a few
catches.

A PAS DE BOURRÉE COURU &
   GRAND JETÉ EN AVANT

SLIDE LEFT FOOT THROUGH 1st

vii. GRANDS JETÉS, EN AVANT AND EN TOUR-NANT ("turning")

Briefly, the sketches above and below show two sorts of *grands jetés* practised by a girl familiar with the movements. Some beginners, however, find it very difficult to get to grips with the basic "mechanics" of these beautiful and effective leaps. The best way of learning to perform them is to follow the sketches very closely—but hardly to leave the ground at first in the leap itself.

B GRAND JETÉ EN TOURNANT

SLIDE

Nos. 1–6 :
COVER DISTANCE
EQUAL TO TWO PACES

TO CONTINUE EXERCISE :
REPEAT MOVEMENT
AS FROM
Sketch No. 3

THEN INTO LEAP

TO CONTINUE EXERCISE :
REPEAT MOVEMENT
AS FROM
Sketch No. 2

CAREFUL

HOW YOU LAND !

7–10 : TRAVEL AS HIGH &
AS FAR AS YOU CAN LEAP

Elevation can be increased directly the student has mastered the actual method. Briefly, the sketches on page 70 show the "preparatory runs" for both types of *jeté*, from which the dancer should gain impetus for both the height and the length of the leap.

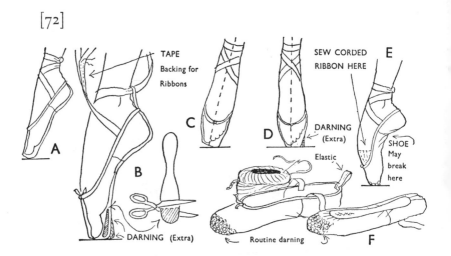

VIII. SUR LES POINTES

i. NOTES ON SHOES AND DRESSES

Some girls rise on their points easily and naturally, and others need to adjust their shoes for comfort. All dancers need to darn the toes of their point-shoes to soften the impact of the toes with the floor, and to lengthen the life of the shoes (see F). A rather flat foot will cause trouble (A), but much can be done to remedy this (B); steps can also be taken to prevent the ankle from turning (C and D). A high arch (E) needs a strong shoe. If the sole breaks, stick one from an old pair firmly inside. Pad the toes with pure animal wool.

On the right are self-explanatory hints for making first *tutus*. The number of frills used may be varied. For examination dresses, the frills are sometimes made of organdie; tarlatan is inexpensive, stiffened net more costly. A *tutu* should be *earned by hard work*—nothing looks more ludicrous than untrained legs under this professional skirt. Students use *tutus* for practice, to get accustomed to the fact that you can't see your own feet through this frilly skirt. They also affect some of your arm positions. And disconcert your partner.

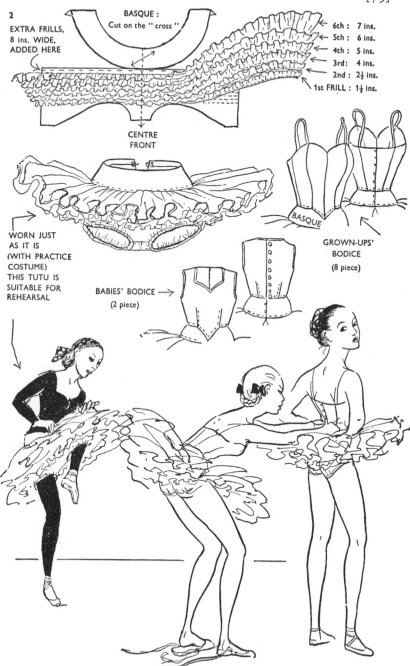

2

EXTRA FRILLS,
8 ins. WIDE,
ADDED HERE

BASQUE :
Cut on the " cross "

6th : 7 ins.
5th : 6 ins.
4th : 5 ins.
3rd : 4 ins.
2nd : 2½ ins.
1st FRILL : 1½ ins.

CENTRE
FRONT

WORN JUST
AS IT IS
(WITH PRACTICE
COSTUME)
THIS TUTU IS
SUITABLE FOR
REHEARSAL

BASQUE

GROWN-UPS'
BODICE
(8 piece)

BABIES' BODICE →
(2 piece)

ii. *FIRST EXERCISES*

The girls on these two pages have a right to be on their *pointes*, as they are all over ten years of age, and have been studying the other exercises in this book regularly for two years. Even so—ALL these exercises are performed with the aid of the *barre*.

A: The correct stance for exercises facing the *barre* (*i.e.*, Figs. A–D inclusive). A3: Wrong stance. *Don't* do this.

Beginners should not hesitate to place a lot of weight on the *barre* at first, to protect the feet from strain until they grow stronger.

A2: For slow *relevés* the knees should be perfectly straight throughout. B: These *relevés* should be performed to brisk tempo, several in each position. C: This exercise, shown here on full point, should be included in the exercises at the *barre*, after the *relevés* shown on p. 35, but on half-point those same *relevés* may be performed here on full point. E1: *Posés* mean "steady"! The movement with the white leg, 2–4, should be as quick as possible. Practise these *posés* slowly and carefully at first, gradually increasing speed.

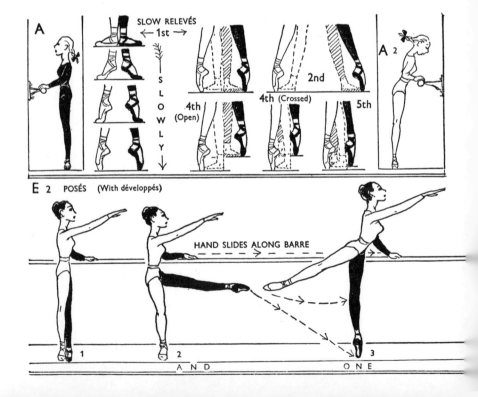

A

SLOW RELEVÉS
← 1st →

S
L
O
W
L
Y

4th (Open)

2nd

4th (Crossed)

5th

A 2

E 2 POSÉS (With développés)

HAND SLIDES ALONG BARRE

1

2

3

A N D

O N E

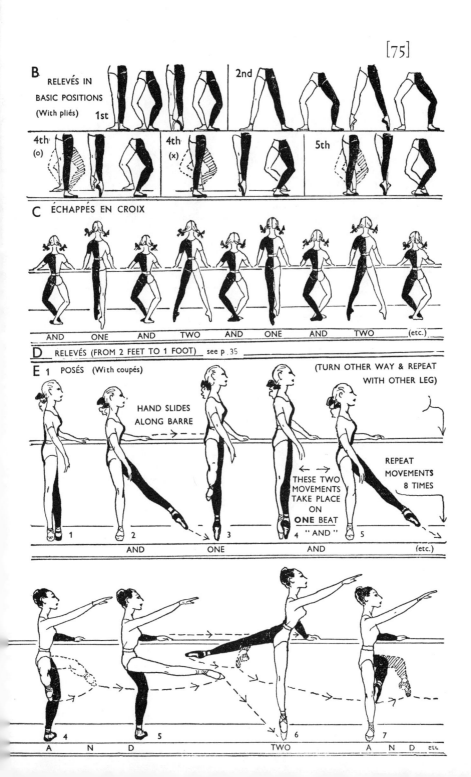

B. RELEVÉS IN BASIC POSITIONS (With pliés) 1st 2nd

4th (o) 4th (x) 5th

C. ÉCHAPPÉS EN CROIX

AND   ONE   AND   TWO   AND   ONE   AND   TWO   (etc.)

D. RELEVÉS (FROM 2 FEET TO 1 FOOT) see p. 35

E. 1 POSÉS (With coupés)

HAND SLIDES ALONG BARRE

(TURN OTHER WAY & REPEAT WITH OTHER LEG)

THESE TWO MOVEMENTS TAKE PLACE ON **ONE** BEAT

REPEAT MOVEMENTS 8 TIMES

1   2   3   4 "AND"   5

AND   ONE   AND   (etc.)

4   5   6   7

A N D   TWO   A N D etc.

| OPENING POSE FOR SIMPLE TARANTELLA | Count : | AND (COUPÉ UNDER) | – |

| SIX – SEVEN (2 HOPS) | – – – | EIGHT (COUPÉ OVER) | – – – |

IX. NOTES ON "CHARACTER"

The sketches above, which have been included to give a general idea of the variety of movement expected from the ballet dancer, show a few steps from an Italian style *Tarantella* of a type suitable for elementary students. Note the "character shoes," which have a low heel.

ONE — — — TWO THREE - FOUR — FIVE
(HIT TAMBOURINE) (3 HOPS) (HIT TAMBOURINE)

REPEAT Fig. 3 in opposite direction

STEP WITH RIGHT FOOT 7 — STEP WITH LEFT FOOT 8 — REPEAT Figs. 7 & 8

ONE - TWO - THREE - FOUR - 5 6 7 8
(STEP . HOP) (STEP & HOP COMPLETING TURN) (2nd TURN)

Under the heading of Character Dancing can be listed all dances of national origin; and mime, or roles requiring a dramatic interpretation such as that of Dr. Coppelius in *Coppélia*, or the Mother in *Giselle*, Act I. Good examples of *demi-caractère* dances are the Scottish and Spanish variations of Swanhilda in *Coppélia*, Act II, which are not authentic national dances but which show a flavour of these countries.

Moral: A good basic training in ballet should enable the dancers to perform anything which may be required of them.

—and finally: "practice makes perfect"—

A. THE MALE
BLUEBIRD. Figs 1-4:
Temps de poisson. Figs. 6-8: entrechât
six de côté (sometimes called entrechât cinq
de voler).

B. THE FEMALE BLUEBIRD. Figs 1-3: échappé à la seconde.
4: relevé à la quatrième devant: 5: retiré: 6-8, développé
& relevé into arabesque. 9-11, pas de bourrée dessous.
Both steps feature stylisation to resemble birds, and are
taken from the two famous "Bluebirds" variations.

WORK HARD

—and ONE *day* . . . . :*—you may do the*
BLUEBIRD PAS-DE-DEUX & VARIATIONS
But it is
NOT FOR BEGINNERS

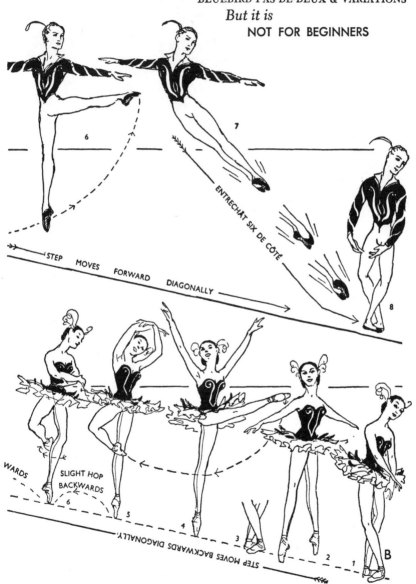

ENTRECHÂT SIX DE CÔTÉ

STEP MOVES FORWARD DIAGONALLY

WARDS   SLIGHT HOP
BACKWARDS

STEP MOVES BACKWARDS DIAGONALLY

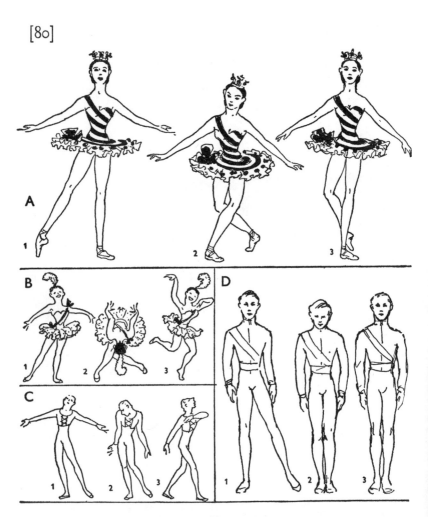

X. MANNERS: CURTSEY AND BOW

The experienced ballerina and *danseur* may vary their bows in accordance with the sort of ballet in which they have just appeared; but beginners should retain their modesty and dispense with tricks which easily appear vulgar and conceited. A, both graceful and dignified, compares favourably with B, which is known as the "yoo-hoo" type of curtsey. C, "the how-lucky-you-are-to-have-seen-me" type of bow; D, a more modest but highly preferable version.

CURTAIN

INDEX

This index has been included, as usual, to help the reader find his way about. It has also been organized with particular reference to the elucidation of French terms. If the reader encounters a term and wishes to know its meaning, the page number given in this index will refer him to the place in which the term is first employed in the course of this book, where he will find an explanation in English and the French verb relative to the term.

[i]

FOR DANCERS ONLY

"Temps de poisson" . . . !

A NOTE ON THE TYPE

This book is set in Electra, a Linotype face designed by W. A. Dwiggins. This face cannot be classified readily as either "modern" or "old-style." It is not based on any historical model, nor does it echo any particular period or style. It avoids the extreme contrast between "thick" and "thin" elements that mark most "modern" faces, and attempts to give a feeling of fluidity, power, and speed.